Living in Avalon: What It's Like to Live on Catalina Island

By

Tiffanie Edwards

Copyright © 2013 by Tiffanie Edwards
All rights reserved. No part of this book may be reproduced or utilized in any form or by any means, electronic or mechanical, including photocopying, recording or by any information storage and retrieval system without permission in writing from the Publisher. Inquiries should be addressed to PO Box 371, Avalon, CA 90704.

Printed in the United States of America
First Edition
ISBN#. 978-1492776604

Author's Note

The names and other identifying details of some people have been changed to protect individual privacy and anonymity.

To Christian and Kevin, for encouraging me to
live my dream.

Contents

1. Chapter One…………………………………….1

2. Chapter Two…………………………………7

3. Chapter Three……………………………..23

4. Chapter Four……………………………….33

5. Chapter Five………………………………...43

6. Chapter Six………………………………….57

Questions & Answers……………………….61

Contact and Community Information………...63

Prologue

Approximately 25 miles off the southern California coast lies a small slice of heaven in a town called Avalon, on an island called Catalina. As a sixth-generation southern Californian, my life was forever changed within moments of first stepping off the boat into this paradise in 2003.

For the next ten years, I fantasized about living in Avalon. I felt like my soul belonged there, though I could never explain that feeling. Many had heard me talk of Catalina, how special it is to me and the strange sense that I would get when I would visit that I am "home." From my first visit, I had the immediate feeling that I knew the place intimately. I stepped off the boat, started walking towards town, looked up at the hills, and stopped dead in my tracks. "Whoa" was what I said. I still cannot explain it, and I have never had that feeling for anywhere else, before, or since. I walked around town that day, like a puppy checking out a new house. I wanted to live there and I knew I would be back.

Over the years, I had been back countless times. On one trip with a friend, we were strolling through streets I had not been down before, and saw an old church. I said aloud, "I'm going to be married in that church someday." Granted, it was not much of a psychic stretch to make that happen when the time came; it was the only thing I insisted on when I remarried a few years later.

As time went on, I had constantly expressed my wish to live in Avalon, not because it is such a pretty place, or because the people are so nice, or because it would be really cool to put my dog in my golf cart and scoot over to the little market for groceries. Avalon has all of that charm and more. Every time I visited I felt like I was looking for something. I admit I had spent endless hours online and in the library researching old photographs, property records, and the genealogy of the people who have lived there. I did not quite know why, but the more I researched, the more interest I gained.

During the previous few years, I had made many changes, gone through positive things, and made a few decisions that did not turn out the way I had hoped. I also realized that it had been my way to pick up something shiny and new and within a few months, suddenly decide it was not for me and move on to the next shiny object. It was not that I was so fickle! After my divorce, I found myself free for the first time in my life to figure out what I wanted, without the restrictions of finances or the needs of my children. Perhaps I should have moved to Catalina in the first place. But it never was the right time. I told myself when the right time came, it would happen. I accepted that it might not be until I was retired, whatever that meant! But I kept asking questions, I kept going back, I kept putting myself out there, making connections and eventually making friends.

Before when I made drastic changes to my life, I did so with the understanding that it was a roll of the dice, it did not have to be forever and that I could always choose again. I am someone who from childhood, never lived in a house for more than three years, always felt disconnected from my parents and family, and consequently, I am perfectly comfortable be-bopping through life all by myself. But as a human being, I had missed a lot! I did not like to admit, that throughout my life, I had never felt a soul connection to much of anything. There was no "family home," my adopted family's lineage was not mine, and my biological parents and grandparents were all now dead. I had my children, and I loved them more than I could love anyone, but they were grown now and we were not attached by a string through their belly buttons.

They say there comes a point in your life where you have to make a choice to do what makes you happy. I was 45 years old, twice divorced, with two grown boys who were on their own. I wasn't struggling but would never get ahead, and it didn't matter to me anymore. I needed to investigate this mysterious, deep longing; I had to live in Avalon.

I have met countless people who feel the same way as I do about Avalon, who wonder what it is like to actually live here. This book is meant to serve as a personal memoir of my experience, as well as a beginner's information guide to relocating to Avalon. If I can live my dream, you can, too.

Part One

Chapter One

Fall, 2012

I needed to sincerely consider how I would feel if I really moved to Avalon. Would the town and the island seem too small? Was housing going to be impossible? Were there any jobs at all? I had a little money saved, so this would be as good a time as any to make the move. The past twenty years had felt like obligations to everything and everyone else; I did not know what the next twenty years would bring. Perhaps in just another ten years, I would look back on my time on Catalina with fondness, even if I were, by odd act of fate, still here.

I had decided to visit again, for a day or two this time. I would take some resumes, my laptop, and some cash. Because information could not be found so easily on the internet, I had planned to check out the community bulletin board for jobs, as well as apartments and rooms to rent.

I did the mental debate: I reminded myself that I was worth the simplest pleasure of living where I wanted to live, even if it only turned out to be for a short time. I considered that all of my experiences from the previous few years perhaps led up to this decision. I reminded myself that there was every chance I would never go back to the mainland, so I should not waste time worrying about what would happen if it did not work out. I was so hesitant to take that first step, fearful of setting my life in motion, yet I felt compelled to keep going. I was in fear of making a mistake, and of making a fool of myself, as though a part of me believed I had no right to do something that would really make me happy. Still, it dawned on me that my obsession would not have been with me for so long if I were not meant to act on it; maybe I wouldn't live on Catalina for the rest of my life, and so what if it wasn't forever?

I woke up the next morning in Avalon. After sleeping just three hours, I felt I had some clarity. I decided to stay a few more days, so I walked down to the post office arcade where the bulletin board posted all the community information, hoping for both the job and the apartment of my dreams to simply be posted. Undaunted that neither were, I decided that I would just do the footwork, and leave God in charge of the results. I applied to the Santa Catalina Island Company, and the woman told me it could be a week or two before I heard anything. I decided to send my resume to the freight line, and to Southern California Edison, since I had worked for them in the nineties. I left it all in God's hands while I also picked up the newspapers. I was taking steps to make my dream come true, and there was a valuable lesson in that for me. I felt my life had possibilities.

This trip had been different; if I was looking for signs, I got them in the most pleasant ways. The woman who owned my favorite vacation rental not only told me it was the best decision I would ever make, she encouraged me to go right over to the Edison plant, introduce myself, and ask for a tour! I was astonished! I had always believed that a potential job candidate does not simply appear at the offices of a major company and ask for the five dollar tour while dropping off their resume! She assured me that things were done very differently on Catalina. Although I never did get up the courage to do as she suggested, the signs kept appearing. One day when I walked into a shop, another customer remembered me from my most recent visit, two months before. When I sat on the patio at C. C. Gallagher's, people would wave, wish me a good morning, and actually use my name!

My best memory of that trip was the day I stopped at Vons for just a few items. The store was crowded and the lines were long. The man in front of me let me cut in front of him, the lady now in front of me jumped out of line to help the checker bag groceries. The cashier was more than happy to hold everyone up while she went to go find a code so I could buy just a half a dozen eggs instead of an entire carton, and then the guy now behind me threw out his phone number so I could get the discount when I realized I didn't have a Vons Club card. The lady bagging groceries even bagged *my* groceries, and remember her transaction was long over by then! I walked out of that store in amazement. I just loved it here!

Five days later, as I waited with a friend to board the ferry back to Long Beach, I became acutely sick to my stomach. It was not anything I had ingested, and I was uncharacteristically agitated and anxious. My friend lightheartedly suggested I simply *stay*, but I had been warned that one does not move to Avalon without either a job or a place to live, and it would not be sensible to move without either secured. I resisted that bright idea, the one that says, "Screw it! I'm going to do what I want to do," because the truth was, this decision was too important to me, and I wanted more than anything for it to work.

The day after I arrived home, another friend sent me a text about me moving over. He assured me that he would check monthly rates at the Hermosa, and that he would help me in any way he could. A week or so later, I rolled the dice and emailed a follow-up to the Island Company about their employment opportunities. I did not know if it would put me over the top, but I felt good about the letter I wrote. It was honest and enthusiastic, and it took me three days to write and edit. I really did not want to make any stupid mistakes, and I was afraid to do it, but I did it anyway. Realizing their personnel office may be closed for Veteran's Day, I did not hold my breath waiting for the phone to ring.

I kept myself busy, living on the premise that I was preparing for the next challenge and life-change. My resolve was occasionally erratic, but my actions were quite intentional. I reminded myself that I had something to offer to my community, as opposed to weighing what I could gain from it. Of course, I could be that "giving person" while living on the mainland, I was just not inspired to bother.

In late March, I got the phone call that would change my life. I was overcome by emotions not limited to tears. Within a week, I would be living in the most special place in the world, a place where many people walked to work, and a vehicle really wasn't necessary but your neighbor was always willing to lend you his. An island where jobs and housing were acquired by word of mouth and your reputation was your reference. A small town where people really, truly cared about each other, the post office in fact, did not deliver and the hospital had not had a planned childbirth in decades. There was no In-n-Out and thank God, no Starbucks. I had never been bored there, and there was an endless list of things I had not seen or done.

I was moving to Catalina with the deep feeling that I was going home. I was not saying I would never leave, but I was saying that when your soul was home, why would you want to? I was not going to worry about how it was going to turn out. It would turn out fine. I had wanted the simple life for years before I even knew that was what I wanted. No one cared what kind of golf cart you drove, or whether you even owned a golf cart. You would be overdressed in high heels and makeup was optional, though I would not push that boundary too much!

As all of my close friends and even many acquaintances knew of my reverence and nearly romantic obsession with Catalina, I received countless messages from friends on both sides of the channel about my "sudden" move. All were positive and supportive, and that was one of the many signs that assured me that it was finally the right time to make the move.

Once I received that phone call, I felt committed to seeing this adventure through to the end, however it turned out. I overnighted my check for the first month's rent, quit the two jobs I was working, put my car up for sale, packed up what I could take with me, and off I went.

Chapter Two

Spring, 2013

It was clear what I had left behind; I had made the decision to give up the Orange County lifestyle that left me feeling as though I had become shallow and brainless. I did not want to spend my time or money on mani-pedis, tanning, eyelash extensions, and one hundred dollar haircuts. I was never going to accept the pain of perpetually waxing the soft spots, or look twenty-one in a bikini again, and I did not care anymore. Keeping the car running had become a constant worry and a financial burden. I did not want to have to put my game-face on to go to the grocery store to impress people I did not really care about, and who didn't care about me. I wanted a certain quality in my life. Meaning, I wanted to know the names of the staff at the bank and the post office, to actually look people in the eye as I passed them on the street, and maybe, to even have a conversation with a few of them.

Within a week of arriving, my life had changed considerably. On my second night, my roommate offered to take me over to the Casino, where they were holding the Annual Conservancy Ball. It was $400 a plate if you included dinner and went in the front door, but if you waited until after ten pm and did not wear your pajamas, it was only ten bucks. It might have been fun, but I was still too exhausted from the move.

After a few nights of deep sleep, all of that rest was starting to make me feel human. On my first Sunday, I had my morning coffee on the front porch, and watched the world go by in golf carts. My girlfriends Lois and Theresa drove by, and asked if I wanted to go to the greenbelt and walk Theresa's dog Cowboy. I thought Cowboy was a girl, because he weighed a dainty ten pounds and looked like a powder puff. However, legend has it that he once took down a Doberman, so I was not going to call Cowboy a girl to his face.

After the greenbelt, we drove to the casino, and watched the Scuba divers. The water was still quite cold so this was not the best time or place to assess future dating prospects. We then went for lunch at Mi Casita, a very good Mexican restaurant. I was asked to help with the CHOICES booth at the Catalina Community Health Fair on Thursday at the casino, as well as their thrift store fundraiser on Saturday. CHOICES is a program that educates and mentors young people so that they can make better decisions about going down the road to drugs and alcohol. Of course, I said I would love to help!

I was also ready to start job hunting. I had said I would work three minimum-wage jobs to live here, but I was beginning to think that would not really be necessary. However, I was willing to go to any length! My definition of success had definitely changed over the years, and the quality of my life had become the most important thing to me. I did not want that pinched, carrying multiple mortgages and car-payments look on my face! Of course, those were never my actual problems, and I also did not want that pinched, working three low-wage jobs look on my face. The truth was I had never needed much to be happy and I felt like I had the support of my friends, none of whom I needed to impress with a fat paycheck or a house on the hill.

When I updated my friends with stories about what I was doing and what was going on here, it was not about "look at me, living in fantasy-land." As I assured them, this was not Monaco. This was about taking a risk to live a long-held life dream. I believed everyone should live whatever life made him or her happy, however that rang true for each individual. I had never believed that life was supposed to be a struggle, though for me, it often had been difficult. I had learned the hard way that if life sucked all the time, it always had and I believed it always would, I was probably doing it wrong! If my quality of life were truly important to me, I would need to do what made me feel content as a person.

Since I was a young girl, I had wanted to be a published writer, and had compulsively written nearly every day of my adult life. However, I had also started and never finished many books on various subjects. I would lose interest or get sidetracked by life and the current book would be put aside to be finished when I received a new burst of inspiration.

So I did what any modern girl would do: I would post on social media the updates about my new life on Catalina, because I loved it here and wanted to share it. A few friends encouraged me to write more, perhaps start a blog, and encouragement was not something I was used to receiving. I started fantasizing again: I would write about the situational happenings about life on the rock, then someday I would be sitting at CC Gallagher's enjoying a ginger beer and playing "Would You/Wouldn't You?" on random guys when suddenly, some passerby with connections would surprise me with the news that a big publishing house wanted me to do a book! Suddenly, I was Carrie Bradshaw in thrift-store shoes and all I would have to do is gather up a few pieces, write a forward, take some photographs that totally misrepresent how glamorous I am, and voila! In my fantasy, I would get a big fat advance and two weeks later Nora Ephron would want to make a movie based on my life.

Then I remembered that Nora Ephron was dead.

But she had her shot, and this was mine. Who cared where it went? Who cared if I misspelt Monaco, or ended a sentence with a preposition? I decided that I would continue to write, without having expectations about the outcome. I did allow myself the entertainment of the fantasy of movie offers. I was going to have to find some way to finance my life on the rock if I did not find work soon.

I was becoming a little worried about my job prospects. On my previous trip, I had been referred to a man who owned a couple of businesses in town, and I had gone to introduce myself. I wanted to let him know that I was now living in Avalon permanently. He enthusiastically shook my hand and told me about a management position he had opening up for one of his businesses. He said he had an ad in the paper, but that he would call me. A few days later, Lois let me know that he had asked about me, and that she had told him to definitely hire me. I really wanted this job and knew I would be good at it, and a full time, permanent job that paid a living wage was difficult to find on this island.

Within a few days, I had a job interview. We were meeting in a restaurant. I was informed by friends that it was to my benefit that I was not an islander, and I was coached on everything from what to wear to how to act, because it was all done very differently in Avalon. All I had to be was competent and willing. It was going to be such a relief not to have to twist myself up into a ball to pull the appropriate persona out of my head. I was excited, but told myself that if it were meant to be, it would happen. While not being emotionally tangled up in expectations about results, it was difficult to forget that my savings were running low and having a job was a rather large part of the solution. I really wanted to get on with my life.

It was not meant to be. I arrived at the restaurant ten minutes early for our interview. I received a text a few minutes later stating that we would have to reschedule because he was stuck in a meeting. He assured me that he would call to reschedule. He never did. A few weeks later, I was riding with Lois when we saw him coming out of the post office. She flipped a U-turn in her golf cart and urged me to go after him. I jumped out and actually ran after him, calling his name! He finally had no choice but to turn around and acknowledge me. He smiled as though we were long-lost friends and shook my hand, assuring me he had just been very, very busy, but that he would call me. Again, he never did. I figured I dodged a bullet on that one, and I like knowing who I am dealing with right from the beginning. Eventually I learned that people could be just as shady here as they were anywhere else. I had been naïve, but I had really believed that a different type of person chose to live in a small town. The solution was to surround myself with better people.

On my third Saturday I suited up and went to the Catalina Island Health Fair at the Casino to help at the CHOICES booth. Although I was grateful to have something constructive to do, I was really thrilled to find myself riding up to the ballroom in the old Otis service elevator, complete with rusty, rickety gate. I was a little intimidated by all the new people I would be meeting that day, but I pushed that discomfort aside. I spent much of the following Saturday sorting clothes at the thrift store, also to benefit the CHOICES program. I was meeting some very interesting and dedicated people, and learning so much.

I was accomplishing a lot, albeit in a very quiet way, but I also had a lot of down time. I was constantly fretting to my roommate Zeke that I was nervous about my financial prospects and of my difficulty in finding a job. Zeke was patiently reassuring, promising that I would be working my butt off before I knew it, so to enjoy the time off while I had it. His words made me feel better, because I had come from working two jobs, and I had never felt like I was off the clock. I was being given room to adjust, along with a lot of encouragement and support. All of that came because of the company I kept. In my circles, it was okay to say "I'm scared things aren't going to go the way I hope, and then what will I do?" There was security in the answers I received: "It will be okay, just suit-up, and show up." "Everything is exactly the way it is supposed to be right at this moment." And the biggest relief of all, "You are not the one who is in control anyway, so just go with the flow."

Although living in Avalon had been more of an adjustment than I had anticipated, the good news was always that I did not have to go back to the mainland anytime soon. It still staggered my mind when I would wake up every morning. My favorite days were when I could go slow, and maybe enjoy a big breakfast of eggs, bacon, hash browns, and sourdough toast. Then I would stroll to my special spot; in a small town where privacy and solitude was at a premium, everyone had one. I used to sit at my spot at the edge of the water on the bay and tempt myself to make the move, imagining what it would be like to really live in such a special town. I now sometimes had a difficult time letting it sink in that I really lived here, but it was starting to get comfortable, like shrink-to-fit jeans.

After more than two weeks in paradise, I had learned how to wear much less makeup and still look like me. I whittled it down to concealer and powder, eyeliner, mascara, and lip stain. I also learned that I did not always need to carry a purse; no matter where I was, I was always right around the corner from my house and could easily drop off anything extraneous and then go on my way.

One afternoon, I went to one of the little shops to buy a few items. When I handed the nice older man my ATM card, he said there was a $10 minimum on ATM purchases, but that $9.40 was "close enough!" He studied my bankcard for a long time before ever so politely handing it back to me. He called me by name, and asked where I was from. When I told him I had just moved from Orange County, he asked if I had found a job yet. When I told him that it seemed to be a rather slow process, he told me not to worry; I would do just fine here. Everyone was so welcoming, positive, and encouraging here, like the family I had always wanted.

That evening, I received a call from Gail, who lives in New Orleans. She would be coming over for a week and wanted to know if I would have time to play when she arrived! She liked to take early walks along the beach and collect sea glass. I thought that was a wonderful idea, because sea glass would make charming Christmas presents. I intended to buy little cork-topped glass bottles off ebay and make Catalina Sea Glass fridge magnets.

A few days later, I went out to Pebbly Beach with Lois. What a fabulous beach to find those treasures like sea glass. Unfortunately, I found that you need good eyesight to hunt sea glass, and I was not a contender. Fortunately, you can still find remnants of tile and pottery from the demolition of the Catalina Clay Products factory, demolished in the sixties. Rumor has it they just bulldozed the whole factory and its contents into the ocean, and ocean-turned pieces still washed ashore. Also fortunate is that original pieces from a private collection are available at Catalina Pottery in the Metropole Marketplace. Also washing ashore to this day are old pieces of dishware from the great Hotel St Catherine, which was built in Descanso Bay after the fire in 1915, but demolished in about 1966. It was hard for me to imagine those huge old hotels, similar in size and scale to the Hotel Del Coronado, being built in a tiny place like Avalon, but that's the way it used to be here...big steam ships, big hotels, and no golf carts...

Within moments of stepping off the boat as an official resident of Avalon. Fresh makeup hid the signs that I had been in tears only an hour before as I boarded.

$100 in barge charges for clothes I never wear!

Saying goodbye to my car. No, I did not look back.

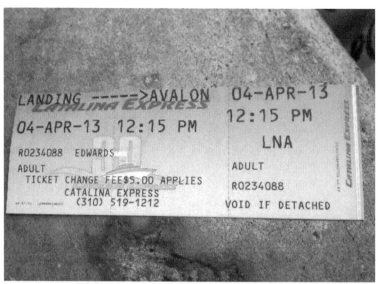

A one-way ticket to the rest of my life!

Transportation between Catalina and the mainland. Or what I now refer to as "the freeway."

My moving truck, Avalon-style!

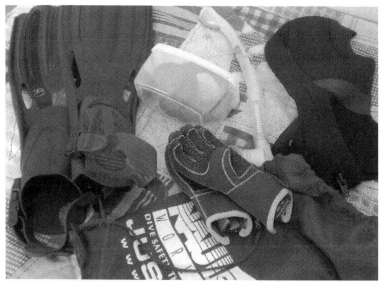
The first things I unpacked were the necessities.

Avalon Meals on Wheels.

What I call Auto Club on the Rock.

The tiniest FedEx truck I have ever seen!

Chapter Three

On the rock, it was perfectly normal to leave one's keys in their golf cart. One morning, a friend woke up to find his cart had disappeared. I asked the first stupid question that popped into my head, "Have you filed a police report?" He replied, "Nah, it'll turn up. There's no place for it to go on an island." I was curious about this attitude! It was just accepted that often on a weekend night, drunken tourists stumbling back to their room from a bar would see the keys in the ignition and decide to take it for a spin. If it was not returned by the time you needed it to go somewhere, you would sit on your front porch and wait for it to drive by. If that failed, you would ask a friend to drive you around and look for it. When this particular missing golf cart could not be found after a few hours, I asked, "If there is no place for it to go on an island, what could have possibly happened to it?" The answer was that sometimes they are driven into the water and left to rust. No wonder some islanders are a bit wary of tourists! The missing cart did eventually turn up abandoned, but the keys were missing, requiring a call to the local locksmith. The owner never did file a police report.

I was often surprised by the behavior of some visitors and was told, "People cross that channel and lose their mind!" Seen every day are people who throw their trash and cigarette butts on the ground and those who openly drink alcohol in town or on the beach. I was often woken from a dead sleep at two in the morning by people yelling and screaming, laughing or fighting, at the top of their lungs all the way back to their room from the bar at the end of a night. There are those that would block traffic walking down the middle of the street instead of using the sidewalks, as well as stop their cart in the middle of the road, to get out to take a photograph. And we had those that would race their rented golf carts down city streets as though they were on a perfectly safe ride at an amusement park. At one time, a guest who was staying in the private vacation rental next to mine walked out onto the front porch at six in the morning and yelled "COCKADOODLE-DOO!" at the top of his lungs, went back inside for a few minutes, then came back outside and did it again.

    We were getting into peak season and the island was coming alive. Residents were picking up jobs left and right and that put everyone in a good mood. Islanders seemed to come in two types: those who were willing to work, often at more than one job and those who did little but hustle, not batting an eyelash to ask for three hundred dollars a week to house sit while you went to stay with your sick mother. There were also the ones who illegally worked under the table while collecting government aid in the form of housing, food stamps, and childcare assistance. The entitlement mentality of some was hardly reflective of the whole as most islanders were good, honest, and hard-working people.

    Early in May, I was hired as a Front Desk Clerk at The Casa Mariquita Hotel. I enjoyed the work, and was able to meet so many people from all over the world. Almost all of our guests were happy to be there, as they were on vacation. I enjoyed hearing their stories and I loved answering questions about the island. My commute was one of the best parts of my day; eleven seconds on foot! I had once been asked if anyone ever uses the word "traffic" on Catalina. Since there is not a single traffic light on the entire island, I answered, "Only when we're talking about "overtown" defined as the mainland. The fact was, I only thought of traffic when I crossed the street from my house to get to work. As in, "this cross town traffic is going to kill me." I thought if I were to be taken out by a golf cart that would be very funny! At least they could say I went out living the life I had wanted to live. Another perk of my job was that at least once a week, we would get phone calls from guests planning to surprise a girlfriend with a marriage proposal on their trip to Avalon! It was so much fun to be a part of the planning, and I loved knowing the secret when the guest and their unsuspecting intended checked in and the proposal story once it was over. The answer was always yes!

By the end of my first month on the job, I had earned a raise in pay, and it was a nice relief. I had been wondering how I was going to eat the following month, but I had learned that things had a way of working out. It took a while, but I had finally learned a few tricks about how to afford food in this town. Bananas seem to be a major staple to residents, similar to the importance of bottled water on the mainland. It was socially acceptable to visit someone's home and help yourself to the bananas and other fruit sitting out on their countertop. There was also a vegetable co-op. Red meat was almost prohibitively expensive, but I knew where you could get a breakfast burrito for $1.99, a burger and fries for $4.50 and coffee for fifty cents. Every Sunday, Avalon Community Church would hold a community breakfast between services, and I had heard the food was very good! And occasionally Meals on Wheels had leftover lunches from the various restaurants around town for three dollars, delivered to our door.

Sometimes, I would get the uneasy sense that I was living in a communist country. There was a definite understanding that some things were simply not discussed. Not much was a secret, but there were secrets nonetheless. By most accounts, alcoholism and drug-dependence was a difficult issue on Catalina. There were no treatment centers or sober living homes to offer support when someone was ready for it. There was one location for Alcoholic Anonymous meetings, but anonymity on this small island was non-existent and created obstacles for those who needed help but were too embarrassed or "high-ranking" to ask for it. The alcohol and drug abuse issue also created a challenge for law enforcement. As a community, we wanted visitors to have fun when they visited. However, when intoxicated people got out of hand, law enforcement was hesitant to issue citations or to make arrests. Arrests cause crime statistics to rise, which threatened tourism.

At the end of May, the town held the "Taste of Avalon" event. I loved that for one dollar per sample I could taste the various offerings at several different restaurants in town. Visitors and residents alike filled the sidewalks along Crescent, chatting as we waited in line and comparing opinions about each restaurant's offering. It was a lot of fun, and the food was great. Also, "Gatsby" was playing at the Avalon Theatre, and what a fitting venue! As a finale to the month, my boss took us on the Flying Fish Tour. I thought I might catch one and fry it up for dinner, but they were not very pretty and I had heard that they were not suitable for eating. The highlight of the tour was the three young men who flashed us their bare bum as the spotlight passed across their boat.

Around the beginning of June, I learned of a most unusual inconvenience of living in Avalon. I woke up one morning to find there was no water running to the saltwater toilets. As this was potentially awkward among mere roommates, I grabbed a pitcher and filled it with tap water a few times, and voila! As it turns out, the toilets did not work quite often. We just kept a pitcher handy and life went on. But this new development caused me to wonder: if one was supposed to drink the water from the toilet tank in an emergency like an earthquake, what were we to do in Avalon? Because I had never seen a water tank in the condition that mine was in, complete with barnacles and Nemo doing the backstroke.

I also had to get used to limited TV channels, as Direct TV was too expensive for our budget, but at least it was available. Local cable meant little more than eighty channels of The Nanny, Golden Girls, and endless Law & Order reruns. No E Network or Bravo. Many residents had Netflix and Hulu accounts to expand their viewing options.

Because I lived on a busy street, a much bigger frustration was the incessant noise of the golf carts that kept me awake at night. I was beginning to get cranky, so I started researching noise machines to help with this problem. After sound-testing several versions, I knew I had to simply accept the noise level, because I could never fall asleep to the sound of a fire, a train passing by, or even the sound of running water. All options were nixed. "Golf Carts" would have to do.

The first thing I saw when I woke up in the morning was the sky, because my windows did not have anything covering them! This made for some interesting floor-level contortions while dressing. As was bound to happen, there was one occasion when I was dressing after a shower, and turned around to see a man working on top of the building two doors away, but I do not think he noticed me. Otherwise, it was nice to see what the weather might be like that day. On many days during this time, I would see clouds or grey sky, which meant another cold day. We were all just a bit tired of the chill and the wind. It was supposed to start warming up, and I looked forward to it. Summer days made me feel alive, and want to do some things I had never done.

On one of my days off, I was able to spend it at a friend's whose family had a vacation condominium over in Hamilton Cove. There was a private beach and swimming pool overlooking the ocean, tennis courts, and a lot of peace and quiet, as they are without the constant buzzing of golf carts. Most of the condominiums are used as vacation rentals, and I was told that it was often teachers who owned them. They would live in the condominium during the school year, and when summertime came, they would rent them out for thousands of dollars a week. This arrangement would cover the mortgage for the year, as well as help finance their summer-long travel plans. Sweet!

By this time, I had been single for almost two years, and I was becoming curious as to how one would meet new people. I did not drink and so did not find bars appealing, but I had also not found anyone who intrigued me. I did not see how one could date privately, as nothing was private in a town this small. A friend who grew up here told me that in Avalon, "you don't lose your girlfriend; you just lose your turn." Gagging through my laughter, I decided I would have to be very, very careful if I decided to date someone. I had to believe that God was working in my life behind the scenes, holding off on certain aspects of my life until I was ready to handle them. I was grateful for all that I had in my life, but I still hoped for a lot: I hoped to be happy here. I hoped to make true friends here. And I hoped to fall in love again.

Progress was being made. Although on this island there were virtually no opportunities for an education beyond high school, I had found some free college-level classes on coursera.com. A new concept in education funded by The Bill and Melinda Gates Foundation, some classes were given for college credit, while others were not, but I began a writing class and signed up for a few other classes that interested me.

I was starting to believe I was living the dream, as the questions in my life had all become so simple: Did I have to go to work that day and what would I wear?

Simple questions made for a simple life. It was not perfect, but I could breathe. I realized that since I moved to Catalina, I never seemed to be aware of what day of the week it was. I not only had time to work at a job I enjoyed, I had time to take care of myself and even to chat with girlfriends on the telephone. I was surprised to hear myself think, "Well, I guess I must be happy!" It was a very unusual state of mind for me, so to celebrate my freedom, I went zip lining.

On nights I wanted a treat I ate at the Lobster Trap. The fresh local lobster served with shrimp stuffing was the best I have ever had, and it was worth every penny. It was a shame it was only available during lobster season! On nights I was too tired to go out, I would carry my dinner home in a box and eat in my room while I studied. On weekend nights, I would go for a walk downtown after dark, and the sidewalks would be full of people. There was often a live band playing on Wrigley Stage in the middle of town. But I preferred the quiet nights, made complete with the relaxed vibe, the sky full of stars that twinkled like diamonds, and the peaceful bay full of boats bobbing in the water.

During special events, such as the Centennial, the city would have a free dinner on the beach for as many as five hundred people. There were often booths all along Crescent, offering an array of delicious food. On those nights, you only had to walk downtown to scope out your dinner and enjoy a little socializing.

Chapter Four

Summer, 2013

It was hard to believe it was June already! I was starting my third month in Avalon, and so much had changed for me, yet I was still having trouble adjusting to the way things were done here. Whenever I had a question, I was always told, "This is Avalon!" As in, get used to it. For one, I found that living in a tightly condensed community such as Avalon had its drawbacks. I had to repeatedly ask my downstairs neighbor to keep his music turned down because it made my floor vibrate and gave me migraines. Soon after, I was woken up two days in a row by someone calling my roommate Zeke about a boat motor he had for sale on ebay. Finally, I asked him, "Is someone calling you at five thirty in the morning about a boat motor? Zeke said, "Yeah, he lives on the east coast." I replied, "Well, tell him you live on the *west* coast."

But I drew the line one day before I left for work. A man walking out of the church next door to our house saw Zeke standing on our patio, and asked if he could use our shower? Zeke's first response was to say yes, but perhaps because I was actually present, he then said, "Let me ask Tiffanie." As I could not see the man's face, I asked, "Who wants to know?"

Zeke: "I've never seen him before in my life."

Me: (Gesturing about my body with my hands) "This is pristine, that is a "naked" room. You would let a total stranger get naked where you get naked?"

Zeke: "Ask and ye shall receive."

Me: (Frankly losing it) "And what kind of a person thinks nothing of asking a stranger if they can come into their home and use their shower? Good luck ever getting him out of the house! They have public showers at the beach for the boaters, he can use those."

    I had to wonder if this really was an Avalon thing, this concept of no boundaries. Later that day, I reminded Zeke of the icky personal things that go on behind a closed bathroom door. I no longer cared if I lived in La-La Land; certain boundaries had to be maintained.

    In the meantime, I had been counting my blessings. I had a job and a place to live. My boss seemed happy with my work and little by little, I was settling in to life on the rock. I could definitely use more money, but I had everything I needed. An old friend from Orange County was coming to visit soon and that did more for my mood than I cared to admit, partially because I was looking forward to getting Michael's perspective on my lingering reservations about whether I had made the right decision to move to Catalina.

Michael was eager to get out of the O.C., and I was eager to get out of town. I needed to touch bases with someone who had known me for over a decade. We stayed at the Catalina Canyon Resort, which is just up the hill but a mile away from the constant noise in town. More than once, we soaked in the Jacuzzi, and just hung out by the pool. For dinner, we took the shuttle into town and ate at the Lobster Trap, which is a great local hang-out. The vibe is so relaxed that as the hostess was trying to figure out where we could sit, other diners invited us to join them at their table!

The next day, we were off to Descanso Beach, one of the best beaches in all of southern California. It is simply beautiful, complete with open-air bar, food service, cushy chaise lounges and cabanas for rent, and even some very nice bathrooms! The party atmosphere on a summer weekend is more than I cared to handle anymore, but it was a beautiful, calm day, and while we enjoyed the scenery, Michael told me, "This was exactly what I needed." His assessed my concerns, concluding that I was doing what other people only dreamt of, and encouraged me to not give it up. A warm beach and a good friend I can say anything to, and I was reminded that all was actually quite perfect in my world. Despite my concerns, after airing my brain out with Michael, I could not help but be reminded that I was practically living the dream.

The glamour wore off when I was humbly reminded of what a small town I now lived in when I had to stand in line at Vons on a Saturday night to buy feminine supplies. It seemed everyone in town was there, and I was mortified, pretending to be too confident to care, yet feeling like a pubescent 13 year-old! "*I'm living the dream,*" I stubbornly reminded myself.

On one of my rare days off, I received an early morning text from my boss saying that someone had stopped by to invite me to a potluck to welcome new residents to the island. She was a friend of the woman who owned my favorite vacation rental, Shelton's on the Island. Well, how sweet! I wondered if that meant I was finally home, because I was beginning to feel that shift. I no longer felt so out of my depth and uncomfortable. Sometimes people would say hi to me by name as I walked through town during the day, and I usually had no idea who they were.

I planned to take Shrimp Caprese Skewers to the potluck, which was being held at the radio station. The event was put together by one of the radio personalities, also a newcomer to the island. I ended up having a great time, although I did not meet Prince Charming. I did meet two new friends, and I was so glad that I did something out of my comfort zone.

By late June, it was clear my luck was changing. The pivotal day started with a bird pooping on me, twice! Then we got so busy at work, I was able to work an hour overtime, and I needed the money. As an added bonus, I did not have time to eat all day, so I surely lost a few unnecessary ounces. Then I found out I would be watching that night's Centennial Fireworks from the bow of my new friend's boat. My boss suggested I go buy a lottery ticket, but I was already feeling lucky enough.

All week the city had been hosting barbeques and other events in celebration of Avalon's Centennial, so I met some friends downtown for dinner. How did the city feed everyone? They laid out tables and chairs all along Crescent and the beach, and everyone would grab a seat wherever they could find one. By this time, I was finding it hard to go hungry in this town, as somebody was always hosting something. I guessed I had put on five pounds in the prior month, but I had probably needed it.

After we ate, we walked my friend's dog, a Dingo mix, along the backside of the Casino and partway to Descanso. We then boarded a dinghy and made our way to the boat. It was dusk, my eyesight was not great, and I was not physically strong, so I thought I might end up in the water by night's end. Alas, I stayed dry, but when the fireworks started, I did not grab my cell phone to videotape it as I wasn't going to risk walking on that skinny little bit on the side of the boat. I accepted that if it was in my destiny to go for a swim I could live with it, but I knew my cell phone could not!

The fireworks show was amazing, truly beautiful. I became quietly emotional but made sure my friend could not tell that by looking at me. I was so proud and honored to even be in town the night of that celebration, let alone be a resident. When the show was over, the cheering of the spectators on land, combined with the horns of the boaters in the harbor, echoed off the hill creating the effect of an amphitheater. I wondered if any of those big plate glass windows in some of the houses shattered during the show that night!

In less than another week, we would be treated to another fireworks show for the 4th of July! The hotel where I worked was completely booked for the holiday, and I was so tired when I got off work some days that I wondered if I was going to make it through the season, though I loved playing a positive role in our guests' vacations. We had a couple on their Babymoon come in on the cruise ship one Tuesday, and Avalon worked its magic. Consider, they left Long Beach on their cruise Monday night, and woke up in Avalon on Tuesday morning. They spent only a few minutes in town, went back to the cruise ship and after considerable argument with the cruise line staff, packed their belongings. They got off the ship to spend their last vacation as childless adults here with us. They said they loved it here that much and felt that this was what they needed before their lives changed drastically forever. I had told them I liked their style!

As the weather warmed up, I made plans to go on a pseudo double date with my new friend. I had decided to call this period in my life my yacht phase. At least I assumed it was just a phase. I had to assure my long-time friends on the mainland that I would not be taking off on any sudden, life-altering cruises around the world on a sailboat! I had an admittedly irrational fear of being cold and wet as I drowned while being eaten by a shark. The ocean was overwhelmingly beautifully to be sure, but for the most part, I felt safer enjoying it from land.

I was so thrilled when I was invited to what was going to be the best Fourth of July party ever, at a girlfriend's home that overlooked Avalon Bay. I had heard the Independence Day fireworks were spectacular, and after the fireworks show we had seen the previous week, I was really looking forward to the evening. I was excited that I was able to be a part of it, and relieved that I did not have to sit in traffic to get home that night. It was a potluck, and I had again planned to prepare my Shrimp Caprese Skewers. In the days leading up to the party, I had to make four trips to the grocery store to get the large shrimp that I needed. I was finally rewarded when I got a tip that there would be an extra barge delivery the night before the holiday.

Living on an island, we just accepted that we could not always get what we needed, even from a grocery chain like Vons. The fact was, it was a small store, and sometimes they ran out of items, especially during a busy week. Bad weather sometimes meant the barge could not run. I was also beginning to understand why residents host potlucks when they entertain. At this time in my life, forty dollars for the three ingredients I needed for the Shrimp Caprese Skewers was not a reasonable part of my entertaining budget. I would have to find a less expensive offering for future On-The-Rock-Get-Togethers, and a family-size bag of Doritos was beginning to sound like a great idea.

There were two additional highlights to our holiday weekend in Avalon. The first was the toilets going out nearly citywide, for the second time in a week. It was my turn to tell our guests at the hotel, "Welcome to Avalon! We'll be right up with a bucket!" The second was the ringing of the chimes tower, located near the Zane Grey Pueblo Hotel. One day when I was in a grumpy mood, it suddenly rang "I'm a Yankee Doodle Dandy" instead of the usual tolling every fifteen minutes between 8 am and 8 pm, as it has since 1925. It was so unexpected I laughed out loud as I walked downtown.

Chapter Five

One of the delights of living in Avalon was the deer that populate the hills above town. One evening, Lois and I went for a drive up past Descanso. As we rounded a corner, there stood a lone deer in the street. We stopped the cart and just watched her while she watched us. Then she came even closer. I tried to get video, but I was only able to get a few pictures. The deer often wandered right into town, looking for water and food. This often meant they would destroy the best laid flower and vegetable gardens, explaining why otherwise pretty houses would sometimes have rather unattractive fencing surrounding the homes.

Towards the middle of July, my computer crashed. It is times like these that you realize that the small-town stand-by of duct tape and some twine were not going to get me out of every bind! Luckily, I still had internet access on my phone, so I put out a mayday on facebook. I will forever be grateful to Serena, for patiently walking me through the crisis! There are computer geniuses in Avalon, but I honestly did not know who they were and I had no time or money to find out.

I was working six days a week, and still taking classes online. The classes helped me to feel like I was at least intellectually expanding my horizons, even if most courses were not for college credit. But between working nearly every day, studying, and other obligations, I found it very difficult to eat properly, and trying to keep it inexpensive was difficult. I normally love to cook, and I would consider it rude to prepare a meal and not invite my household "family members" to eat with me. But the truth was I could not afford to feed anyone but myself. For a brief while, I was sticking to fruit, but it was expensive and the quality was sometimes uncertain. I will say I have consistently found the best pears in Avalon, as they were usually ripe and juicy. However, one day the regular pear bin was on sale, and it was easy to see why. The fruit was overripe and beginning to spoil. Since I just wanted one pear, I decided to pay the extra money and go organic. It was a revelation! Once I got all the fancy stickers off, it tasted just like...a pear.

One of more fascinating aspects of Avalon was the history of the buildings and the various types of architecture. Since many of the structures were built in the early 1900's and some in the 1800's, much of the housing was not up to current building codes. In my apartment, the entrance is into the ground level foyer, and the living space is up a flight of stairs. I had been warned about the stairs, yet I had tumbled down them more than once. The widths of the steps were just too narrow, and it was easy to misjudge. Yet it was my own fault for nearly breaking my neck. I had gone down the stairs too quickly, or in the dark. In Avalon, one would not think of demanding that your housing be brought up to code. We liked to do things the old-fashioned way: By turning the light on and watching where we were going.

My whole week was made when I learned Audra and Serena were coming for a visit, along with their daughters! We had been friends since the fifth grade, and we now kept in touch through facebook. We were all counting the days. They were due to come in the early afternoon, after I was off work. When all the girls got off the boat, there were hugs all around, but screaming like spastic teenagers had never been our style.

The girls stopped to freshen up in the public restrooms at the mole while I waited outside. Eventually, Serena made it out, but it was taking everyone else an inordinate amount of time. Serena went in to see what the delay was and asked Audra if everything was all right. By the look on her face, apparently it was not. There had been two completely naked women in the bathroom, fondling each other out in the open. Of course, Audra had said something, but they just looked at her and kept on. I was mortified as their teenage girls were present, and Avalon is a very safe, family-oriented town. Those women had been lucky I had not been the one to catch them.

The younger girls took a snorkeling tour while the Moms went to Bluewater Grill for appetizers. Bluewater Grill now stands where Armstrong's had been located, in the old ferry terminal building on Crescent, right on the water. I had loved Armstrong's and had held my wedding reception there because the food was so good. However, I was familiar with Bluewater Grill in Newport Beach and felt it was a reputable replacement once Armstrong's had closed. The afternoon was gorgeous and sunny, and I wanted Audra and Serena to relax and soak up the atmosphere. They only had the afternoon, and at one point, they were both glued to their cell phones. That was one classic way islanders can spot tourists, as they run their empire from paradise. Later in the afternoon, we took a walk over to Descanso and briefly witnessed a wedding on the beach, complete with a barefoot wedding party!

From time to time, other friends would debate coming to Catalina. Either they had never been here or hadn't been in years. We were all at that age where we were conditioned to go to Vegas by default when we wanted a weekend getaway. But I was the new ambassador for Catalina among my friends! "Vegas screams, Catalina whispers and rubs your toes," I would tell them. I wished I could invite them to my spacious hilltop home overlooking the beautiful bay, but my modest accommodations were more akin to living on a boat, complete with roommates and a rather embarrassing bathroom.

Groupon and other websites had some wonderful deals, not only for ferry transportation and hotel accommodations, but also for excursions that even residents could take advantage of from time to time. I scored a $19 snorkeling tour at the Avalon Underwater Dive Park at Casino Point. Several years before, I had taken the semi-submersible Underwater Sea Tour, and it was so breathtakingly beautiful under the water that I was inspired to get my SCUBA certification the previous summer. I went to classes for a month, but ultimately could not be certified due to a medical limitation. Since I owned all the gear, I decided snorkeling would be my new favorite thing to do. Unfortunately, while I was able to complete the tour, I felt very uneasy in the open ocean. I was surprised and disappointed, but at this point in life, I just accepted my limitations, even when they were all in my head. I decided I would stick to swimming pools as they are less physically taxing and there are usually fewer sharks to worry about.

    One great benefit of working in a hotel was that you often heard about events before the general public, because the information is being filtered through you to promote. On one lucky day, a lady delivered fliers promoting a tour of the historic Tuna Club. There were only sixty tickets available, so I picked up the phone and immediately made my reservation. I felt so lucky to be able to tour this building that millions had only ever walked past. I did not know if it was true, but I heard they still did not let women inside unless they were employed there. Politics aside, I loved the tradition. I had hoped to take pictures of the interior, which may have explained why they didn't want women inside! I had also heard that the walls told stories, and that even Winston Churchill had been a member during his lifetime.

    For a long time, I had also wanted to stay at William Wrigley, Jr.'s Avalon home, which was now a hotel, called the Inn on Mt Ada. It was a bit out of my price-range, but I learned they accepted reservations for breakfast or lunch. Reservations needed to be made twenty-four hours in advance, and breakfast was $25 per person while lunch was $35 per person. I had been told that the home was built with a saltwater bath option, and I was curious to learn what other luxurious amenities were considered necessary back in 1921 when the home was built. I had always loved old houses, and someday I hoped to stay there so that I could get a sense of what it might have been like to live there.

    Life was cracking for me by August. I had found a second job at one of the higher- quality clothing stores in town. The extra money would make it possible for me to attend a wedding overtown in October, and most important, to visit my grandson in Arizona when he was born in early December. I would also qualify for an employee discount, very much welcomed because shopping for clothing could be a challenge in a small town on a small island. There was only one shop that sold decent undergarments. For my taste in women's clothing, Avalon Bay Company had the best selection and the prices were reasonable. In some other stores, I had to wonder how they justified charging $50 for a dress I had seen for $10 at a swap meet. Most people stocked up on basics when they went overtown at Target and Wal-Mart. There were two thrift stores in town, but they were small and the selection was hit or miss. Luckily, fashionable clothing really was not a high priority here, and for that, I was grateful!

Catalina Coffee & Cookie Company, where those in the know get their morning joe! They open at 5 am!

The gorgeous patio area in the Metropole Marketplace.

At least once a week, a cruise ship comes to town! Avalon pulls out all the stops to show our guests a good time!

A gorgeous Avalon sunrise.

Catalina Zip Line Eco Tour...an absolute must when You visit Catalina!

Descanso Beach Cabanas

Descanso Beach from the open-air bar.

My favorite picture of Avalon Bay.

Our charming cross-town trolley.

Chapter Six

I had lasted nearly six months in Avalon, and had never regretted my decision to come to Catalina. Not once had I thought of packing it in and going "home." As far as I was concerned, I *was* home.

It seemed to be a common belief that residents, native or not, lived in this simple community because we did not know any better. The truth was most of us lived here because we *did* know better! Another assumption was that the town needed someone to come over and show the islanders "how it's done." They decide we needed a Starbucks or a McDonalds. The truth was, if the people who lived here wanted those things, we would have chosen to live anywhere else in the country. If those types of businesses existed here, the town of Avalon and the island would lose its unique charm that made it so special.

Once I began writing this book, people asked me what *I* knew about living in Avalon, since I had just arrived. My answer was that I could only write from the perspective of my own experience. If someone else wanted to write about *their* experience, I think the world would welcome the information. There was never enough public information about this fabulous paradise, the true lifestyle, and especially the history…the real history, not the Disneyland version. I was still fascinated by the Banning era, for example. It was next to impossible to get access to this information, and the difficulty further stoked my endless curiosity about this magical island.

Something mysterious about this island has fascinated millions of people for well over a century. It was William Wrigley, Jr.'s dream to "make Catalina a playground for all, rich or poor, youth or aged." Whether the magic is inherent to the diversity of the land, or the history of the island and its people, there will always be more to learn. Catalina and the town of Avalon have a unique story that continues to unfold with every passing year. I believe that it is vitally important that current and historical information become more easily accessible to the public.

The information provided in this book is my beginning contribution to that goal. Although I did not know what compelled me to return to Catalina time after time, year after year, I do know that six months ago, I had two life dreams. And Catalina has now made both come true.

Part Two

Questions & Answers

Q: When is Avalon getting a Starbucks?

Hopefully, never. Much of the magic of Avalon lies in the fact that most of the local businesses are Mom & Pop operations. They are owned and operated by the local people who live here; and many have been family-owned for generations.

Q: What if I lose my wallet or cell phone?

In Avalon, you have at least a 50/50 chance of having your items returned to you, but there are no promises. As on the mainland, you must take responsibility for securing your belongings as any prudent person would. That said, it is not unusual to come across a post such as this on the community bulletin board:

"If someone recognizes this bag it was found by City Hall. go to the front desk to pick it up."

Q: How expensive is food?

Due to the transportation costs of shipping everything over to the island by barge, groceries are about 30% higher on Catalina as on the local mainland. We never go shopping without our Vons Club card!

Q: Where do you get your water?

Most of our fresh water supply is rainwater, collected in reservoirs outside of town. Our freshwater supply is very precious, and residents do not waste it. The tap is turned off during tooth brushing, and one does not dawdle in the shower! Vehicles are washed only occasionally, and even the size of the bucket you can use to wash your golf cart is regulated city ordinance.

Q: What do locals do on a daily basis?

Locals often work at more than one job. We raise our families, attend little league, and community functions. For fun, we have all the water activities, as well as hiking and camping. Going to the movies are a big hit. The locals participate in many other activities that may be unique to the community: Prom Walk, Bingo on the Beach, Movies on the Beach, fundraisers, Taste of Avalon, the activities are endless!

Contact
And
Community Information

The phonebook for the entire island of Catalina is about 70 pages in length, weighs just a few ounces, and is delivered to residents' post office boxes. The area code for Catalina is traditionally 310, but is also sometimes 424. The prefix is 510. It is understood that most telephone numbers are known to begin with "310-510," so when being referred to a phone number, you will often be given just four numbers, as it is assumed you already know the area code and prefix. For example, the telephone number to Catalina Medical Center is simply "0700."

The most common question is, "What does it cost to live here?" The answer is it costs about the same as Los Angeles, or Orange County, California. That means a two-bedroom apartment will cost at least $1500 a month, with higher ranges being common.

Apartments Complexes

Avalon has three apartment complexes that I know of, Bird Park Apartments, Eucalyptus Gardens Apartments, and Tremont Street Apartments

Banking

There is one bank on the island, US Bank.

Church

There are several churches in town. Avalon Community Church, Catalina Bible Church, St Catherine's Catholic Church, and a Kingdom Hall of Jehovah's Witnesses.

Courthouse

There is no longer a courthouse in town. If you get a jaywalking ticket, you now have to factor in a roundtrip ferry ticket, plus ground transportation, into your budget.

Curfew

When I was a kid, the curfew for minors was when the streetlights came on. In Avalon, the curfew is either 11 pm, or 12 midnight. No one really knows for sure. Yes, this means there are very young children running around late at night unsupervised.

Education

I have been asked if children go to school on Catalina Island. Of course they do! Schools are all part of the Long Beach Unified School District. There are two pre-schools. If you wish to further your education while living on Catalina Island, your only options are online or to move off the island.

The library is a branch of the Los Angeles County Library, and although it is tiny, it is open most days of the week, and items can be ordered through the inter-library loan program. Although they do have free internet access, do not plan on tying up a computer for longer than a few minutes.

Employment

The vast majority of jobs are tourism-dependent. However, this is a real city, with a City Hall, a Sheriff's and Fire Department, a Museum, parking enforcement, Animal Control, a Southern California Edison plant, and a cable company, to name a few. Some people end up here by accident, such as a job transfer. Many do not stay, as they feel the island is not good fit for them culturally or socially. Many people came for a visit, fell in love with the island, and stayed. Most are working class. Most of the very truly wealthy just have homes here and do not live here full-time. Seasonal jobs are found with the Island Company, as well as tour companies, hotels, restaurants and personal care facilities. Some jobs come with decent pay, medical benefits, or various standards of housing.

Electronic Supplies

Radio Shack: Small, but has the basics.

Groceries

Avalon has two grocery stores, Vons and Vons Express. Each carries somewhat different items, and they are both the size of a convenience store! Due to transportation costs, prices are about thirty percent higher than on the mainland. Therefore, one would never go grocery shopping without their Vons Club Card. Buying when items are on sale and using coupons are common methods locals use to stretch their grocery budget. Others periodically take the ferry to stock up on bulk purchases. It should be noted that produce cost and quality is difficult to predict. There is a community garden for fresh produce, but the details on that are unknown at this time. Many people utilize the service Farm-Fresh-To-You, but the service does not technically deliver to Catalina. Through word-of-mouth, we have a contact person on the island who arranges for the shipment and then delivers it to your door! The locals buy fresh seafood at Avalon Seafood at the end of the pier, the Lobster Trap, and a few other locations.

This is the Vons egg case after a holiday weekend, empty. Islanders stock up for days like this!

Hardware:

Chet's, located in the postal arcade. They also have a decent selection of general household goods.

Healthcare

Catalina has one hospital, Catalina Island Medical Center, which was formerly known as Avalon Municipal Hospital and Clinic. Located at 100 Falls Canyon Road. PO Box 1563 (310) 510-0700. The emergency room is open 24 hours a day, although it is often necessary for seriously injured or ill patients to be airlifted to mainland facilities. The hospital has *minimal* in-patient facilities. They have physical therapy, wound care, and skilled nursing for long-term medical care. Many full-time residents make use of the clinic that provides primary care including hearing and vision services, prenatal care, pap smears, well child checks, immunizations, and vaccinations. Standard insurance plans are accepted, including Medi-Cal and Medicare. *Due to the high risk nature of childbirth, the hospital does not perform deliveries. The hospital is not equipped to deal with the range of complications possible during a difficult childbirth. Expectant women are advised to go to the mainland two weeks before their due date.*

Once a year the town holds a health fair at the Casino Building. Doctors and other health professionals set up booths in the ballroom, and residents can be assessed for everything from high blood pressure to diabetes, bone density to skin cancer. Lab work is performed at an average cost of $25 per test, much less than paying out of pocket to your standard lab overtown.

Prescription medicine seems to be a difficulty. When I arrived in Avalon, I had been taking an inexpensive thyroid medication that cost on average $8.00 per month without insurance. That same prescription cost $31.00 in Avalon! Solutions include having the medication mailed from a larger pharmacy on the mainland.

If all of that fails, Avalon has one cemetery, and end-of-life services are coordinated through Midgley Gardenside Mortuary 310-510-1406. When someone dies, their bodies are sent overtown to prepare them for burial or cremation, and the remains brought back to the island for interment or inurnment, if this will be the final resting place. Only Catalina Island residents can be buried in the cemetery.

Housing

Housing is expensive, scarce, and difficult to find. If you are in a position to buy, it is no more difficult to buy in Avalon as it is on the mainland. However, with some property, you will not own the land.

If you are a renter, you have the usual options of renting a single-family home, which would cost you at least $2000 a month in the off-season. There are a few apartment buildings, and those with studios start at $800. There are many hidden and tucked away, non-traditional apartments, some with shared bathroom facilities down the hall. You can also rent a room, either year-round or seasonal.

After some time on the island, I have learned how low-wage earners can afford to rent…subsidized housing, which has its own qualifications and a long waiting list.

facilities. The hospital has *minimal* in-patient facilities. They have physical therapy, wound care, and skilled nursing for long-term medical care. Many full-time residents make use of the clinic that provides primary care including hearing and vision services, prenatal care, pap smears, well child checks, immunizations, and vaccinations. Standard insurance plans are accepted, including Medi-Cal and Medicare. *Due to the high risk nature of childbirth, the hospital does not perform deliveries. The hospital is not equipped to deal with the range of complications possible during a difficult childbirth. Expectant women are advised to go to the mainland two weeks before their due date.*

Once a year the town holds a health fair at the Casino Building. Doctors and other health professionals set up booths in the ballroom, and residents can be assessed for everything from high blood pressure to diabetes, bone density to skin cancer. Lab work is performed at an average cost of $25 per test, much less than paying out of pocket to your standard lab overtown.

Prescription medicine seems to be a difficulty. When I arrived in Avalon, I had been taking an inexpensive thyroid medication that cost on average $8.00 per month without insurance. That same prescription cost $31.00 in Avalon! Solutions include having the medication mailed from a larger pharmacy on the mainland.

If all of that fails, Avalon has one cemetery, and end-of-life services are coordinated through Midgley Gardenside Mortuary 310-510-1406. When someone dies, their bodies are sent overtown to prepare them for burial or cremation, and the remains brought back to the island for interment or inurnment, if this will be the final resting place. Only Catalina Island residents can be buried in the cemetery.

Housing

Housing is expensive, scarce, and difficult to find. If you are in a position to buy, it is no more difficult to buy in Avalon as it is on the mainland. However, with some property, you will not own the land.

If you are a renter, you have the usual options of renting a single-family home, which would cost you at least $2000 a month in the off-season. There are a few apartment buildings, and those with studios start at $800. There are many hidden and tucked away, non-traditional apartments, some with shared bathroom facilities down the hall. You can also rent a room, either year-round or seasonal.

After some time on the island, I have learned how low-wage earners can afford to rent…subsidized housing, which has its own qualifications and a long waiting list.

You must apply directly with the apartment management for assistance. Generally, available housing is posted on the bulletin board in the post office arcade, but are most often found by word of mouth. Otherwise, you can subscribe to the Catalina Islander Newspaper for updated listings on a weekly basis. Some people live on their boat, but there are restrictions and costs involved. Shower facilities are available for boaters for a small fee.

Laundry

There are at least two Laundromats: A single load of laundry will cost at least $3.00 to wash and about $2.00 to dry, and that is for the smallest load.

Movies

Avalon Theater: One movie a week.

Moving & Storage/Shipping

Large items that cannot be sent through regular mail are shipped over via the freight line. Items are shipped by weight, and they have a cost calculator on their website.

Catalina Freight Line
100 W Water St
Wilmington, CA 90744
(310) 549-4004
catalinafreight.com.

Moving & Storage
Catalina Transfer
310-510-2287

Moonstone Office & Storage
310-821-2528

Newspapers- published weekly on Friday

Avalon Bay News
117 Whittley
310-510-1500

Catalina Island Newspaper
101 Marilla
310-510-1500

Pharmacy:

Leo's. Also has basic makeup supplies.

Post Office

The post office does not deliver, so there are no mail carriers on Catalina! Everyone on the island must go to the post office located in town to pick up their mail. Each residence is allotted one post office box. Mail sent to long & short-term visitors, boaters, and others can be sent "General Delivery." Fed Ex delivers to your door.

Radio Station

KISL 88.7.

Real Estate/Vacation Rentals

Shelton's on The Island
PO Box 1226
Avalon, CA 90704
310-510-1707
www.sheltonsontheisland.com

Catalina Island Real Estate
119 Sumner Ave Suite K
PO Box 326
310-510-3000
www.4cire.com

Hamilton Cove Real Estate
116 Clarissa
310-510-0190
www.hamiltoncove.com

Hunt & Associates Realtors
119 Clarissa PO Box 2148
310-510-2721
www.catalinagetawayrentals.com

Catalina Island Vacation Rentals
119 Sumner Ave
(310) 510-2276 (855) 668-2487
catalinavacations.com

Smoking

Smoking is allowed in Avalon with the exception of some common sense restrictions. Not a single hotel allows smoking. Aside from the usual reasons, fire is a huge threat to Avalon. One misplaced cigarette butt could decimate the entire town, as well as the island. Consideration and common courtesy by using the ashtrays provided around town, and refraining from leaving cigarette butts on the ground, is greatly appreciated.

Sobriety Resources

The Alano Club/AA Meeting room is currently at 230 Metropole, and will be relocating in the summer of 2013 to Avalon Community Church. Current Updated meeting schedule can be found at the base of the Green Pier, and on Facebook under "Catalina Alano Club" in the "About" section. ***There are very few other resources for people with drug and alcohol issues on the island, but recovery can be found if you want it.*

Transportation

Two ferry lines currently serve Avalon and Catalina Island with regular daily service from Newport Beach, San Pedro, Long Beach, and Dana Point. If you are a resident of Catalina, you can qualify for a commuter pass, which lowers your cost per one-way ticket on the ferry to about $20. Restrictions apply, such as a minimum length of residency before you qualify for the discount. You can rent a helicopter to come over, or you can swim. You can also float your own boat, and even live on it! Contact the proper authorities as to restrictions and mooring costs. The Catalina Airport-In-The-Sky is 10 miles out of town.

The main method of transportation in Avalon is by golf cart. Golf carts are probably used because of their size and cost. I would be interested in knowing *how* golf carts became the primary form of motorized transportation in Avalon, and it should be noted that they are not permitted out of town. I wish they would go electric; they are so damn loud, like buzzing mosquitos all day, every day! A golf cart is not required unless you find it necessary to suit your needs. A local trolley runs on a fixed route, or you can hire a taxi, as residents can apply for a reduced rate. Mopeds, scooters, bicycles and the Heel-Toe Express are also common options.

It is very difficult to get a permit to have a full sized vehicle in Avalon. The city has its own strict permit program that local vehicle owners must comply with, in addition with the usual requirements imposed by the statewide Department of Motor Vehicles. The waiting list for a permit for full-size vehicles is rumored to be between 14-30 years. If you purchase a business that already has full-size vehicle permits issued to it, those are normally transferred to the new owner as well, but this has to be approved. There are also different permits issued to vehicles for use primarily in the interior.

The cost of gasoline is among the highest in the nation, commonly and currently over $7.00 a gallon. Luckily, golf carts are not too expensive to purchase, but that is relative. Registration and insurance are minimal compared to the mainland. The DMV comes to Avalon once or twice a year to process vehicle registrations and conduct behind the wheel driving tests. Interim drivers are only issued licenses for golf carts until a behind-the-wheel test can be conducted in a full-size vehicle in standard traffic conditions on the mainland. There is one gas station in town, located on Pebbly Beach Road.

Further questions can be directed to:
tiffanie.edwards@facebook.com

Made in the USA
San Bernardino, CA
10 July 2016